IN THESE SHOES WE WALK COLORING BOOK

In these Shoes We walk coloring book

Published By Maria Madden-Williams

Published ByMaria Madden-Williams
Publishing Consultant & Book Design

SOPHISTICATED
PRESS

To every grieving Mother, Father, Grandmother, Grandfather, Sibling, and the entire family... God is with us as we walk in these shoes. He will never leave or forsake us God will be with us until the end of time as this journal comes to an end put your hand over your heart and release this out of your mouth you are always in my heart and smile. I love you all be blessed. This walk given to the strong your testimony will help others.

Maria Madden-Williams

Blessed are those who mourn, for they shall be comforted.
Matthew 5:4

He healeth the broken in heart
and bindeth up their wounds.
Psalms 147:3

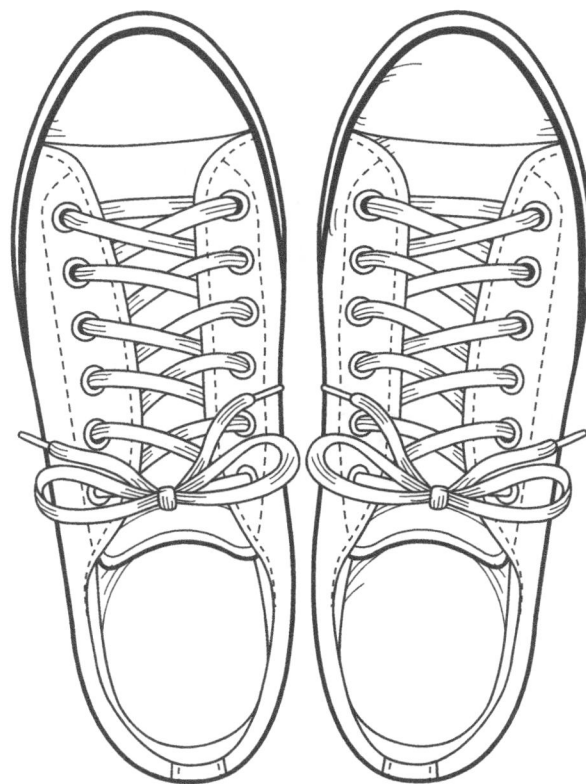

Reflections

God has strengthened our walk.

_____

_____

_____

_____

_____

_____

_____

_____

_____

_____

_____

_____

_____

_____

Peace, I leave with you my peace I give unto you
not as the world giveth give I unto you.
John 1427

Reflections

We are not alone in this walk. God is with us.

_____

_____

_____

_____

_____

_____

_____

_____

_____

_____

_____

_____

_____

_____

_____

My flesh and my heart faileth: but God is the strength of my heart, and my portion forever. Psalms 73:26Peace, I leave with you my peace I give unto you not as the world giveth give I unto you. John 14:27

Reflections

Our memories are forever.

_____
_____
_____
_____
_____
_____
_____
_____
_____
_____
_____
_____
_____
_____
_____

Trust in the Lord with all thine heart and lean not unto thine own understanding. In all thy ways acknowledge him and he shall direct thy paths.
Proverbs 3:5-6

Reflections

Death can not destroy our bond
with our children.

_____

_____

_____

_____

_____

_____

_____

_____

_____

_____

_____

_____

_____

_____

_____

_____

Come unto me all ye that labour and are heavy laden and I will give you rest. Take my yoke upon you and learn of me. F or I am meek and lowly in heart and ye shall find rest unto your souls. For my yoke is easy and my burden is light.
Matthew 11:28-30

Reflections

This Love is forever.

_____
_____
_____
_____
_____
_____
_____
_____
_____
_____
_____
_____
_____
_____
_____

For we walk by faith not by sight.
2 Corinthians 5:7

Reflections

Always in my heart.

_____

_____

_____

_____

_____

_____

_____

_____

_____

_____

_____

_____

_____

For God so loved the world that he gave his only begotten Son, that whosoever believeth in him should not perish but have everlasting life.
John 3:16

Reflections

I can still see your smile and it makes me smile.

_____

_____

_____

_____

_____

_____

_____

_____

_____

_____

_____

_____

_____

_____

"In the English language there are orphans and widows, but there is no word for the parents who lose a child."
— Jodi Picoult

The Lord is close to the brokenhearted and saves those who are crushed in spirit.
Psalms 34:18

Reflections

I give all your worries to him because he cares for you. 1Peter 5:17

_____

_____

_____

_____

_____

_____

_____

_____

_____

_____

_____

_____

_____

_____

The name of the Lord is a strong tower;
the righteous run to it and are safe.
Proverbs 18:10

Reflections

The joy that you brought me is forever imprinted in my heart.

_____

_____

_____

_____

_____

_____

_____

_____

_____

_____

_____

_____

Seek the Lord and his strength, seek his face continually.
1 Chronicles 16:11.

Reflections

Forever in my heart.

_____

_____

_____

_____

_____

_____

_____

_____

_____

_____

_____

_____

_____

Cast all your anxiety on him because he cares for you.
1 Peter 5:7

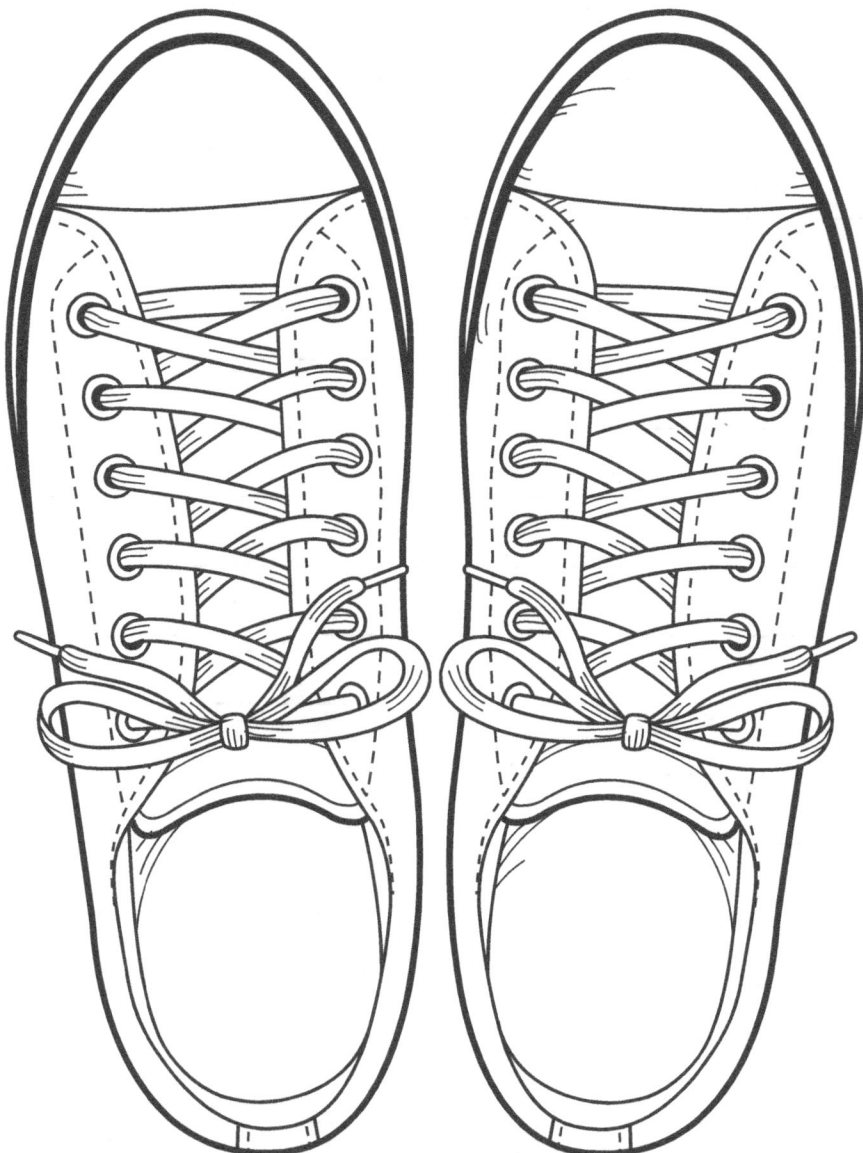

Reflections

The laughs, I still hear and I smile.

_____
_____
_____
_____
_____
_____
_____
_____
_____
_____
_____
_____
_____
_____

The Lord is a refuge for the oppressed, a stronghold
in times of trouble.
Psalms 9:9-10

Reflections

Every time that I heard you say Ma
will always remain.

_____

_____

_____

_____

_____

_____

_____

_____

_____

_____

_____

_____

_____

_____

_____

My presence will go with you, and I will give you rest.
Exodus 33:14

Reflections

Even though you are not physically here I still feel your love.

_____
_____
_____
_____
_____
_____
_____
_____
_____
_____
_____
_____
_____
_____

Cast all of your burden on the LORD and
He will sustain you.
Psalms 55:22

"My feet will want to walk to where you are sleeping
but I shall go on living."
— Pablo Neruda

Reflections

My grace is sufficient for you. For my power is made perfect in weakness. 2 Corinthians 12:9

_____
_____
_____
_____
_____
_____
_____
_____
_____
_____
_____
_____
_____

It is the Lord who goes before you
He will be with you.
Deuteronomy 31:18

Reflections

The Lord is my shepherd, I shall not want.
Psalms 23

_____

_____

_____

_____

_____

_____

_____

_____

_____

_____

_____

_____

_____

_____

_____

In the world you will have tribulations but take heart I have overcome the world.
John 16:33

Reflections

Be still and know that I am. God Psalms 46:10

_____

_____

_____

_____

_____

_____

_____

_____

_____

_____

_____

_____

_____

_____

_____

_____

_____

Whenever I am afraid, I will trust in you.
Psalms 56:3

Reflections

For nothing will be impossible with God.
Luke 1:37

_____
_____
_____
_____
_____
_____
_____
_____
_____
_____
_____
_____
_____
_____
_____
_____
_____
_____

Draw near to God and he will draw near to you.
James 4:8

Reflections

Pray without ceasing. 1 Thessalonians 5:17

_____

_____

_____

_____

_____

_____

_____

_____

_____

_____

_____

_____

_____

_____

_____

Blessed are those who mourn for they shall be comforted.
Matthew 5:4

Reflections

Little by little, grief slowly fades.
But love always burns brightly.

_____
_____
_____
_____
_____
_____
_____
_____
_____
_____
_____
_____
_____
_____

"There is no right way to grieve; there is only your way to grieve and that is different for everyone."
— Nathalie Himmelrich

We know you'd be with us today
If heaven wasn't so far away.

Reflections

The pain passes, but the beauty remains.
– Renoir

_____

_____

_____

_____

_____

_____

_____

_____

_____

_____

_____

_____

_____

_____

_____

There are some who bring a light so great to the world that even after they have gone, the light remains.

Reflections

Earth has no sorrows that heaven can't heal.
– Thomas Moore

_____

_____

_____

_____

_____

_____

_____

_____

_____

_____

_____

_____

_____

Notes

_____

_____

_____

_____

_____

_____

_____

_____

_____

_____

_____

_____

_____

_____

Notes

_____

_____

_____

_____

_____

_____

_____

_____

_____

_____

_____

_____

_____

_____

Notes

_____
_____
_____
_____
_____
_____
_____
_____
_____
_____
_____
_____
_____
_____

Notes

_____

_____

_____

_____

_____

_____

_____

_____

_____

_____

_____

_____

_____

_____

Notes

Notes

_____

_____

_____

_____

_____

_____

_____

_____

_____

_____

_____

_____

_____

Notes

Notes

_____

_____

_____

_____

_____

_____

_____

_____

_____

_____

_____

_____

_____

_____